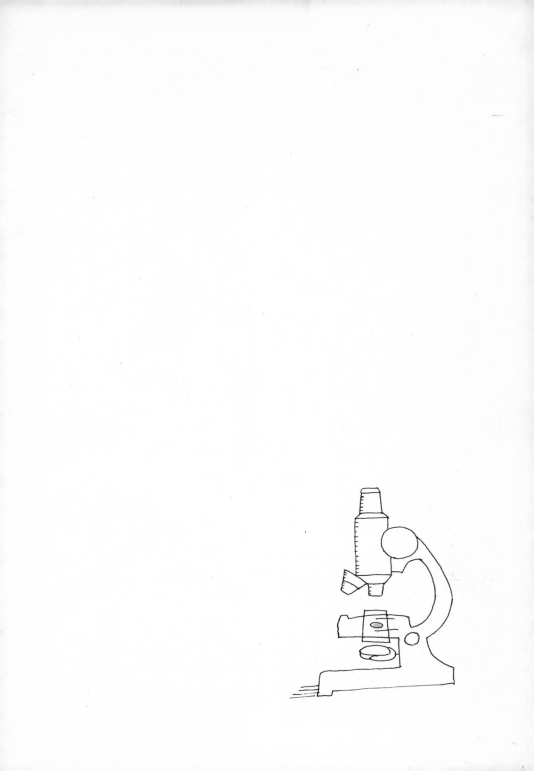

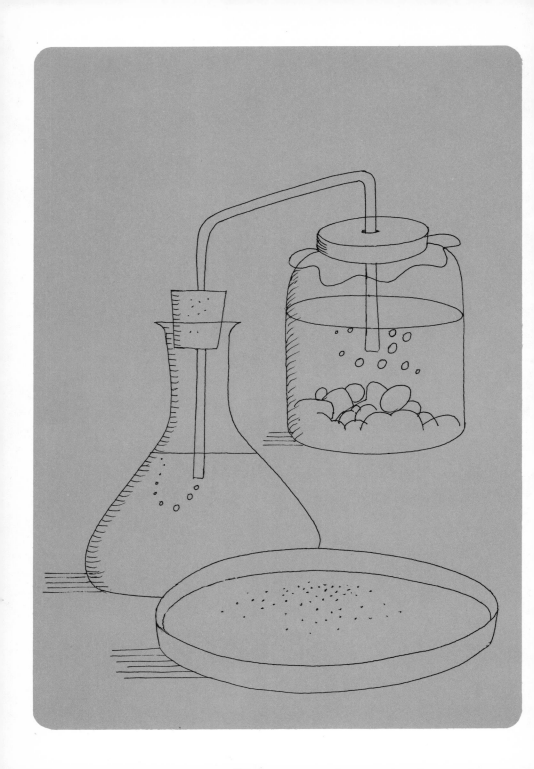

Microbes
are something
else

by A. Harris Stone
and Irving Leskowitz

ILLUSTRATED BY PETER P. PLASENCIA

PRENTICE-HALL, INC.   ENGLEWOOD CLIFFS, N. J.

To curiosity—

Tho it kills cats,

it creates scientists.

Microbes Are Something Else
by A. Harris Stone and Irving Leskowitz

© 1969 by A. Harris Stone and Irving Leskowitz

Illustrations © 1969 by Prentice-Hall, Inc.

Library of Congress Catalog Card Number: 71-84753
Printed in the United States of America • *T*
13-580951-7

Prentice-Hall International, Inc., London
Prentice-Hall of Australia, Pty. Ltd., Sydney
Prentice-Hall of Canada, Ltd., Toronto
Prentice-Hall of India Private Ltd., New Delhi
Prentice-Hall of Japan, Inc., Tokyo

CONTENTS

INTRODUCTION

For as long as man has been on the earth, he has been affected by organisms he never knew existed. These organisms are so small that they cannot be seen without the aid of a microsope. For this reason, they are called microorganisms or, more simply, microbes. All microbes have one characteristic in common—they are extremely small and therefore invisible to the naked eye. In all other respects microbes vary greatly from one kind to another. There are microbes that are plants, some that are animals, and others that are bacteria, yeasts, molds or viruses.

Microbiology, the study of microorganisms, began about 300 years ago. Through the study of microbes, men have made many discoveries about food production, the causes and cures for diseases, the functioning of cells and other problems important to the welfare of man.

What is a microbe? To describe microbes physically is simple. Most microbes have bodies that are made up of only a single cell. This single cell can carry out all the activities needed to keep the organism alive and reproducing. Not long ago, it was learned that microbial cells function in much the same way that the cells of other organisms do. A human liver cell, a yeast cell, a plant cell and a bacterial cell are similar in many ways. There are differences among them to be sure, but certain basic chemical and biological activities are performed by all of them. Therefore, through the study of microbes we can learn a lot about all cells and more about ourselves.

About 150 years after microbes were discovered, it was learned that they could be either useful or harmful. Some, like yeasts were found to be responsible for the brewing of wine and beer. But others, certain bacteria for example, caused serious diseases in man. There is a saying that "The squeaky wheel gets the oil," meaning that those making the most noise get the most attention. Among the microbes, those making the "most noise" are the ones that cause diseases. Naturally enough, these microbes received most attention; so much in fact, that for a long time it seemed as if the only microbes ever studied were those responsible for diseases. Because of this, people began automatically to associate microbes with diseases. They came to believe that all microbes were dangerous to humans; the ways in which microbes were useful were overlooked.

By 1900, many of the diseases caused by microbes were under control and microbiologists began to pay attention to the helpful activities of microbes. Of the thousands of species of microorganisms, there are at most only a couple of hundred species that are harmful to man. The bacteria and other microbes that are beneficial are of far greater importance to us than are the ones that cause disease. In fact, if it were not for the activities of certain species of microbes, life as we know it today could not exist.

There are several species of bacteria that are essential to the continuation of plant and animal life. Man and all other animals receive their food directly or indirectly from plants. Plants need nitrogen in order to grow. Even though there is plenty of nitrogen in the air, plants cannot use it unless it is combined with oxygen and converted to nitrates. Bacteria in the soil are responsible for this change. By their chemical activity, they combine nitrogen from the air with oxygen to form the nitrates needed by plants. Thus our lives depend on the activity of these soil bacteria. No nitrates, no green plants; no green plants, no animal life.

There is a recipe for rabbit stew that starts "First catch a rabbit. . . ." To do experiments with microbes you must first catch a microbe. This is very easy to do, since microbes are literally everywhere. All you need to catch them is the right "bait"; that is, the right kind of food for growing microbes. And that is where this book begins. . . .

THE HAPPY MEDIUM

What changes can be seen in a mixture of sugar, water, gelatin and a beef cube that are allowed to stand at room temperature for several days?

Does varying the amount of each substance in the mixture have any effect on what is seen? What effect is seen if agar (see next page) is used instead of gelatin?

MIXTURE NUMBERS

	1	2	3	4	5	6	7	8	9	10	11	12	13
Beef Cubes	2	2	2	2	1	1	1	1	0	0	0	0	?
Sugar (tsp.)	½	0	0	½	½	0	0	½	½	0	½	?	?
Gelatin (tblsp.)	1	1	0	0	1	1	0	0	1	1	0	?	?
Water (oz.)	3	3	3	3	3	3	3	3	3	3	3	3	3

A growth *medium* is any mixture of substances that will support the growth of microbes. The basic food needs of microbes—of *all* organisms, in fact—includes raw materials for growth and repair, energy sources and vitamins. Materials for growth and repair are obtained from proteins, fats or carbohydrates. The energy source is usually a carbohydrate, such as sugar or starch, but proteins and fats may also supply energy. Vitamins are needed in much smaller amounts than any of the other food substances, but are just as necessary for the proper functioning of the organism.

In addition to proteins, carbohydrates, fats and vitamins, growth media often contain a substance called agar. This substance, which is obtained from a seaweed, causes the medium to set, or gel, so that it has the consistency of a firm gelatin pudding. Such a medium is called a solid medium. A medium which does not contain agar, or some similar substance, is called a liquid medium. Solid media are used in order to obtain pure cultures of bacteria. Each type of medium, liquid or solid, has its special uses, and both will be used in the experiments that follow.

Whether or not a particular microbe will grow in a given medium depends upon the microbe. Some microbes are quite finicky about their food and will only grow on certain media. Although there are many different kinds of microbes, there need not be many different kinds of media. However, certain media are satisfactory for the growth of only one or two different kinds of microbes.

What microbial food requirements are supplied by the beef cubes? What requirements are supplied by gelatin? Were vitamins present in the medium you prepared? Was it necessary to use water in the medium?

SLIDE MAKING

Slide making is an important technique in the study of microbes. The procedures shown below are a guide to the preparation of slides for microscopic examination.

1.

Place a drop of water and microbes on a slide—spread it around and allow it to dry. Gently heat the slide for a few seconds. You have just made a smear.

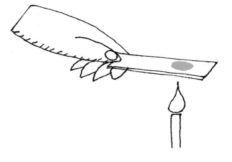

2.

Cover the smear with a few drops of crystal violet solution or iodine solution.

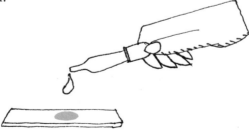

3.

Dip the stain-covered slide in a
glass of water. Change the water
and dip again. Allow the slide to
dry.

4.

Examine the stained
smear with the aid of a
microscope.

What can be seen when microbes are observed under
a microscope? Are there differences in color, size and
shape?

Have patience—focusing a microscope and finding
the microbes takes practice and time.

STERILIZATION

What happens to a batch of medium that has been boiled, covered and stored in a warm place for a day or two?

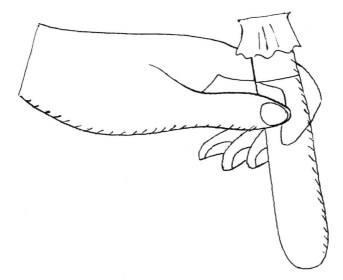

What happens if the medium is treated in the same way but left uncovered? Does the same thing happen to a batch of medium that has been covered and heated in a pressure cooker for half an hour? WARNING: Ask an adult to help you with the pressure cooker.

Sterilization is the process by which an object or environment is made free of all living organisms. There are many ways in which sterilization may be accomplished, but the methods most commonly used involve heat, chemicals or filtration.

Chemical methods of sterilization include using substances that are poisonous to microbes. However, one problem in using such substances is that they may prevent the growth of microbes later on. These substances

can be useful though. Some of them may be poisonous
to one type of microbe but not to others, in which case
they have a special value. For instance, a microbiologist might have a sample containing two species of
microbes. Suppose one of these species is inhibited or
poisoned by some substance that is not harmful to the
other species. The microbiologist could then prepare
a medium containing this chemical. In this medium
one species would not grow but the other one would.
One chemical of this type is crystal violet. Compare the
microbial growth in two tubes; one containing a medium
with crystal violet added, the other containing the same
without crystal violet.

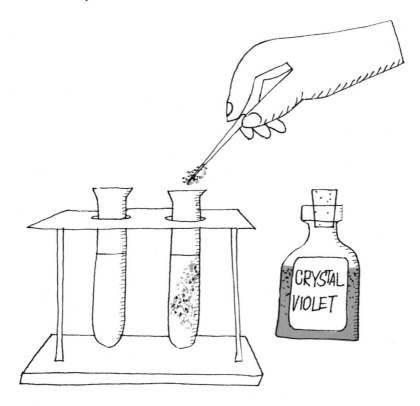

TEMPERATURE AND MICROBES

A box, such as the one shown below, may be used to control the temperature at which microbes are grown.

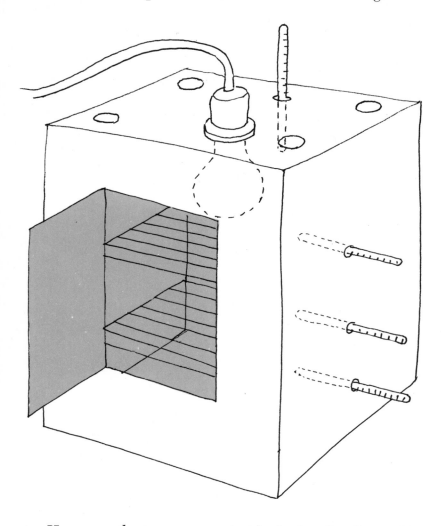

How may the temperature inside the box be changed? Should this box be kept in the coolest place available?

What happens to you when you are very cold? You probably shiver or get "goose-pimples." These reactions are ways your body has of trying to prevent further cooling. What happens when you are very warm? By perspiring, your body is able to cool itself. Therefore, as you can see, your body is able, within limits, to adjust to temperature changes. Microbes are not able to do this and so they are at the mercy of temperature changes in the environment.

The procedure for growing microbes is simple. First, a medium is prepared. Then the medium is *inoculated;* that is, microbes are placed on or into it. The last step is *incubation*, which consists of placing the inoculated medium in a temperature-controlled container to encourage growth.

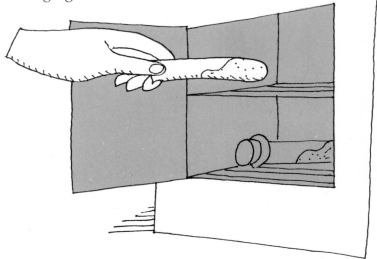

Is there a "best" temperature for the growth of microbes? What differences can be seen among inoculated tubes of a medium that are incubated at different temperatures in the incubator?

THE ACID TEST

Does adding vinegar to the medium affect the amount of microbial growth that follows inoculation? Does the addition of baking soda have the same effect? How about pickle juice? Tomato juice?

The condition, acidic or basic, of the medium can be determined by the use of litmus paper.

Is there an optimum acidity or alkalinity for growth? What effect does adding varying amounts of vinegar have on microbial growth?

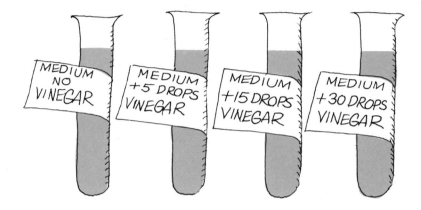

An alkaline solution may be made by adding one teaspoon of baking soda to a glass of water.

SWEET AND SALTY

How well do bacteria grow if salt is added to the growth medium? Does the amount of salt in each tube of medium have any effect on the amount of bacterial growth?

Does sugar have the same effect as salt?

The salt concentration in a growth medium is important for the growth of microbes. Is there a limit to how much salt is beneficial to the organism? What happens to the microbes found in pond or lake water if salt is sprinkled into the water? Can you observe any change in their behavior?

Is the same effect seen if cells of an *Elodea* plant are treated the same way? Do the cells of the skin of an onion "shell" respond similarly to the salt treatment?

WHERE THE MICROBES ARE

What can be seen on the surface of some sterile growth medium that has been exposed to the air for a few minutes and then incubated? How does the exposure time affect what is observed?

Does it make a difference if the medium is exposed in the bathroom instead of the living room? Outdoors instead of indoors?

There is no place on the face of the earth where bacteria have not been found. Wherever microbiologists have searched for them they have been discovered—in rivers, lakes and oceans, in fields and in forests.

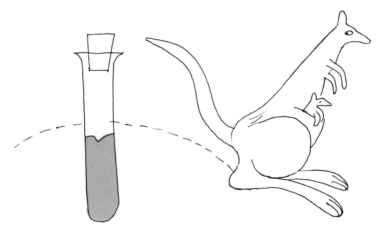

Microbiologists studying the distribution of microbes discovered that many species of bacteria found in soil in one part of the world were also found in soil in other parts of the world. For example, the bacterium, *Bacillus cereus,* is found in the soil in Kansas, in Italy and in Australia. This widespread pattern of distribution is typical of many microorganisms, but it is not true of any other kinds of organisms. The species of corn grown in Kansas is not native to Italy or Australia. Similarly, kangaroos are not found anywhere outside of Australia, except in zoos. What accounts for the distribution patterns of bacteria, plants and animals?

SOIL—HOME FOR MILLIONS

A soil suspension may be made by adding one tea-spoonful of soil to a quart of water and shaking the mixture vigorously. How many different kinds of microbes can be found by spreading a drop of the suspension on a plate of medium and then incubating the plate?

Are the same results observed if soil samples from different places are used?

How many microbes are there in a teaspoonful of soil? This question is not easy to answer, but with the aid of a few simple techniques and a little arithmetic, a fairly accurate estimate can be made.

Transfer a measured amount of soil suspension from one tube to the next, mixing the contents of each thoroughly before making a transfer to the next tube. This is called preparing a serial dilution. If one drop of a soil suspension is added to nine drops of water the new concentration of soil is $\frac{1}{10}$th of the original suspension. If the same 1 to 9 mixture is repeated five times, the soil concentrations in successive tubes will be (1) 1 part per 100, (2) 1 part per 1000, (3) 1 part per 10,000 (4) 1 part per 100,000, and (5) 1 part per 1,000,000.

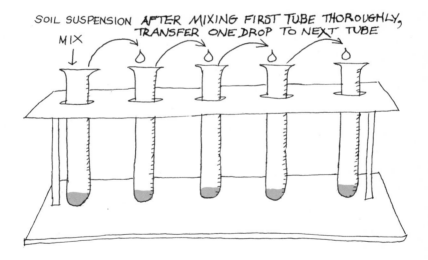

SOIL SUSPENSION AFTER MIXING FIRST TUBE THOROUGHLY, TRANSFER ONE DROP TO NEXT TUBE

MIX

How many microbes would grow on a plate spread from the tube containing the one part per million concentration of soil?

LIFE IN A POND

Is the water in a crystal-clear pond free of living organisms? What can be seen if samples of clear water from several different natural sources are examined without the aid of a microscope? With a microscope? Does allowing the samples to stand at room temperature for several days have an effect on what is seen?

What animals and plants would have been seen in the area in which you live if you had been around to make observations one million years ago? Five hundred thousand years ago? One thousand years ago? Last winter? Last week? Yesterday?

Are any kinds of organisms observable in a sample of pond water after it stands for five days that were not present on the day of collection? After ten days? Some general shapes and forms of organisms that you may look for are shown here. *A Guide to the Study of Fresh Water Biology* by Needham and Needham, may be helpful in doing this study.

ANAEROBIC GROWTH

Does sealing a tube of bacteria and medium prevent the bacteria from growing? Adding methylene blue indicator is helpful in determining the kind of reaction that is taking place.

WARNING: Melted paraffin is useful in sealing the tube, but BE CAREFUL! Melted paraffin is flammable and can burn the careless experimenter.

How long can you hold your breath? Thirty seconds? A minute? Certainly not longer than two minutes. With very few exceptions, animals must have oxygen or they will die. However, there are many microbes that can live and grow in the complete absence of oxygen. Such organisms are called anaerobes.

As the microbes grow, they form products that change the acid-base condition of the medium of growth. Are these products responsible for what happens to the methylene blue? What happens if water and methylene blue are heated together? What happens if a jar half-full of this cooled mixture is shaken vigorously? What substance is missing from the heated mixture? How does the shaking of the mixture in air restore the substance? What can be seen if an acid or base is added to the methylene blue solution? Is methylene blue an indicator of pH? What does methylene blue indicate?

GROWTH INHIBITION

Do substances that stop the growth of molds also stop the growth of bacteria? Can yeast cells grow where molds cannot? Do yeast cells grow in a growth medium that has been treated with a fungicide?

Fungicides can be purchased at drug stores where they are sold as treatment for athlete's foot.

One of the most revolutionary discoveries made by man was how to preserve certain foods. This knowledge made it possible for man to store foods for those times when it became scarce.

What happens to a mixture of molasses, water and yeast, that is allowed to incubate at room temperature for two days? Does the same thing happen if the mixture has been boiled for ten minutes before incubation? Does adding a large amount of salt to the mixture have the same effect as heating does? Does the addition of a large amount of sugar have the same effect? Does adding cooking herbs, such as dill, mace, thyme or oregano have any effect?

WARNING: ASK AN ADULT TO HELP WITH THIS ONE!!

GERMICIDES

What can be observed if detergent is added to an inoculated tube of medium before the tube is incubated? How does the growth in this tube compare to the growth in the same medium without detergent? Do substances such as mouthwash, disinfectants and antiseptics have the same effect as detergents?

Does the germicide's ability to kill bacteria vary with the concentration? Does it vary with the temperature?

A great many substances can kill bacteria, but not all of them are used. For example, concentrated sulfuric acid is an extremely effective germicide, but it is just as good at charring wood, rubber, plastic and human skin. The germicides most frequently used are those that kill bacteria but do no damage to people or objects. The effectiveness of germicides is determined by comparison with a standard germicide. Microbiologists have selected as the standard of comparison a substance called phenol, or carbolic acid. In low concentrations (2% or less) phenol is suitable for use in treating cuts and bruises; in higher concentrations (2–5%) it can disinfect objects, but is harmful to skin.

Compare the germicidal effectiveness of mouthwashes, antiseptics and detergents with that of a 2% solution of phenol.

CAUTION: AN ADULT *MUST* SUPERVISE THIS EXPERIMENT BECAUSE PHENOL IS A POISON.

SUNLIGHT

What happens to bacteria that are spread on a plate of growth medium, exposed to strong sunlight for a period of time, and then incubated? What effect is seen if half the plate is covered by a piece of cardboard during the exposure period?

Sunlamps reproduce certain characteristics of the sun's rays. Does exposing a plate inoculated with bacteria to the rays of a sunlamp produce the same effect the sunlight did? Does the degree of inhibition vary wth the exposure time? Does the degree of inhibition vary with the distance between the sunlamp and the plate?

CAUTION: THE RAYS OF THE SUNLAMP CAN BE VERY HARMFUL TO SKIN AND EYES—BE CAREFUL! ASK AN ADULT TO HELP YOU WITH THE EXPERIMENT.

Visible light is only one of many different forms of radiant energy. Other kinds include X rays, ultraviolet, infrared, television, radio and radar waves. What effect do these forms of radiant energy have on microbes? What happens if a plate inoculated with bacteria is exposed to the surface of a TV tube, with the picture on, for a period of time and then incubated? What effect is seen if several layers of aluminum foil are placed between the TV tube and the plate during exposure? What happens if the TV set is turned on but the picture is "blacked out" during exposure?

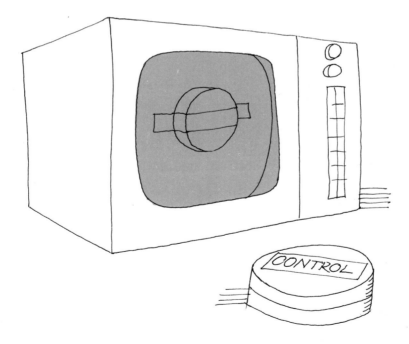

PRODUCTION OF PENICILLIN

Rotten oranges are an excellent source of a mold called *Penicillium*. The mold grows on the orange as a greenish, fuzzy mass. What effect does *Penicillium* have on bacteria mixed into a warm growth medium and allowed to solidify? "Spot" the *Penicillium* as shown.

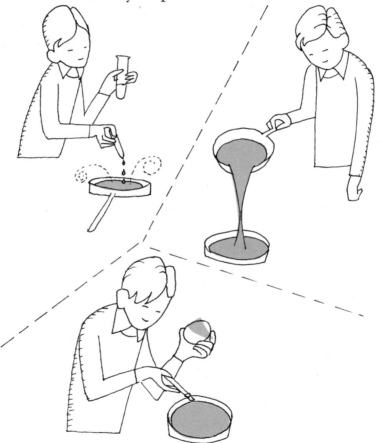

Does *Penicillium* affect different kinds of bacteria in the same ways?

Penicillium is a mold that produces a substance called *penicillin*. This chemical, which is a waste product of the mold, is useful to man. Penicillin inhibits the growth of certain bacteria and for this reason is called an *antibiotic*.

Penicillin can be separated from *Penicillium* simply by straining the medium in which the mold has been growing for about a week. Such a medium can be made by putting *Penicillium* from a rotting orange into pasturized apple juice. The penicillin can be separated from the apple juice by straining or by allowing the juice to evaporate.

Does the penicillin collected in this way have the same effect as the mold itself? Does varying the concentration of the penicillin affect the results? Does heating the penicillin before adding it to the medium have any effect?

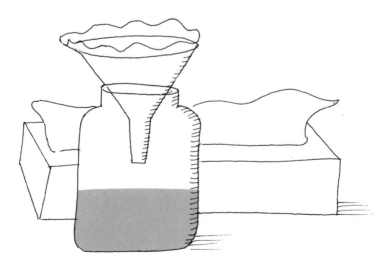

PASTEURIZATION

The pasteurization process is used to decrease the number of bacteria in milk. Has the pasteurization of the milk you buy been effective? What change can be noticed if methylene blue is added to several different milk samples and the mixtures are sealed and incubated at room temperature?

Does the bacterial content of the milk *before* it is pasteurized have any effect on how many organisms remain alive after pasteurization?

What is the relationship between the rate of color change of methylene blue and the number of bacteria in milk? How rapidly does the methylene blue change color in samples of fresh milk? Milk that has stood at room temperature for a day? Buttermilk? A solution of yogurt in water?

Is the rate of color change different if the samples are refrigerated?

STARCH DIGESTION

What effect do bacteria have on starch? This can be determined by using starch instead of sugar in the medium. Streaking bacteria on the surface of a sterilized plate of solid starch medium will be helpful in finding the answer.

What happens if iodine solution is mixed with starch? With sugar?

Certain substances are classified as carbohydrates, the two most familiar being sugars and starches. Carbohydrates are the major source of energy for most microbes. In this respect, microbes are like most other organisms. They may get energy from any of several different kinds of carbohydrates. In obtaining energy from carbohydrates, microbes form a variety of end products, quite different from the original substances in both structure and reaction to various tests.

Whether or not a given microbe can utilize a particular carbohydrate depends on its ability to produce certain chemicals called *enzymes*. Each enzyme digests, or breaks down, one particular substance. If a microbe does not have the specific enzyme that digests a particular carbohydrate, that carbohydrate cannot be used by the organism.

The enzymes produced by microbes are similar to those produced by other kinds of organisms. For example, certain bacteria produce an enzyme that digests potato starch, and this enzyme is similar to one present in human saliva.

What happens if iodine is added to a mixture of saliva and grated potato that has been allowed to stand in a warm place for a short time? Does the same thing happen if a suspension of bacteria is substituted for the saliva?

FERMENTATION

The action of yeast on molasses produces several new products. One of the products is alcohol; another is a gas. What happens when this gas is passed through a solution of calcium hydroxide (called lime water)?

Does varying the amount of yeast in a given amount of molasses and water change the rate at which the gas is produced?

What is the gas produced by the fermentation of molasses by yeast? One way of identifying any substance is to compare its reactions with those of known substances. When baking soda and vinegar are mixed, carbon dioxide is given off. What results are seen when carbon dioxide is bubbled through limewater? Does it seem reasonable to identify the gas produced by fermentation on the basis of this one comparison?

Scientists seek as much information as possible when trying to develop ideas about their observations. In order to identify the gas produced by fermentation, it may be helpful to collect a large amount of that gas and subject it to *several* tests. The apparatus shown here may be used to collect the gas produced by fermentation. Can the gas produced by the reaction between baking soda and vinegar be collected in the same way?

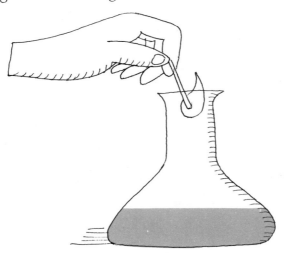

What happens to a lighted candle or match that is plunged into the gas produced by the fermentation? Into the gas produced by baking soda and vinegar? What happens to wet litmus paper placed in either gas?

ANOTHER FERMENTATION

What happens when dry yeast pellets are added to a mixture of table sugar and water? Beef bouillon and water? Apple juice? Salt and water?

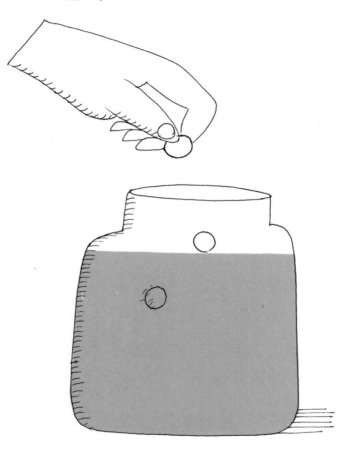

What kind of substances do yeasts ferment? Into which taste group do the fermentable substances fall— bitter, sweet, sour or salty?

The rate at which gas is given off during fermentation is an indication of the rate at which the fermentation is proceeding. This rate depends upon several factors. One factor that you may have already discovered is the concentration of the fermentable substance in the medium. Another factor is the temperature of incubation. The fermentation rate may also be affected by the presence of certain substances. The apparatus shown below can be used to determine the fermentation rate. How rapidly does the liquid move up the tube during fermentation?

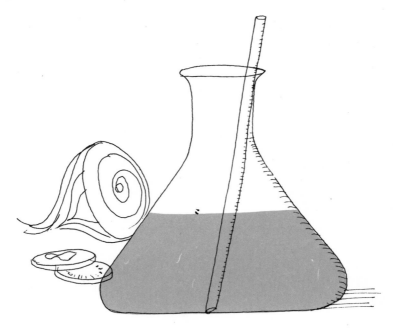

What effect does adding onion juice to the medium have upon the rate of fermentation? Does the addition of copper pennies have any effect on the rate of fermentation?

ALCOHOL

What are some of the properties of the products formed by the action of yeast on pasteurized apple juice? The new products will be formed if a tablespoon of yeast is added to a pint of pasteurized apple juice and allowed to stand in a cool place, loosely covered. How long must it stand before a change is noted?

Is there a difference in the odor before and after fermentation takes place? Does the color change? Is the taste the same? One measurable change that may have occurred can be determined by using a weighted, corked test tube with a pencil stuck into the cork. Does the pencil float higher in the liquid before or after fermentation has taken place? Does the test tube-pencil apparatus float at the same level in water? In water that has rubbing alcohol added? Does the amount of alcohol added to the water change the level at which the pencil and tube float? Does letting the apple juice ferment for a longer period of time change the level at which the pencil and tube float?

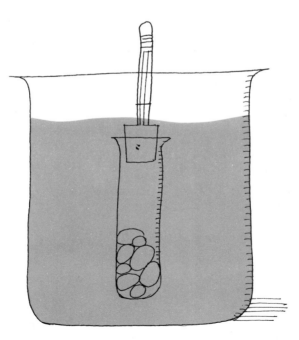

YEAST BUDDING

What can be seen in a mixture of yeast, sugar and water that has been standing at room temperature for about an hour? An easy way to make this observation is to place a drop or two of the mixture on a microscope slide, *gently* place a cover slip over the drops and make observations under a microscope from time to time. Do not *drop* the cover slip onto the mixture; doing so will trap air bubbles in the preparation and these may be mistaken for yeast cells.

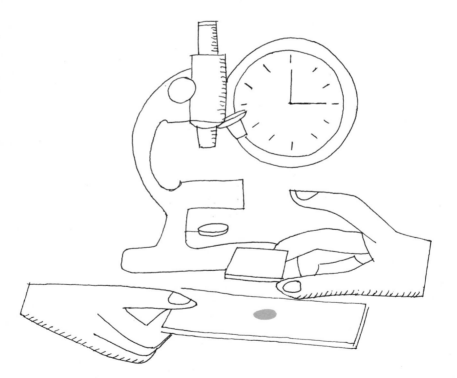

Most microbes reproduce by *fission*, a process in which a cell divides to form two equal-sized new cells. In yeast, a slightly different type of fission called *budding* occurs. In budding, the cell does not divide to form two equal-sized cells; instead the cell forms a small copy of itself, a bud, that remains attached for some time. The bud grows larger and soon produces more buds. A single yeast cell may produce several buds at a time. Budding is a very efficient way of reproducing. Starting from a small amount of yeast, it is possible for a large amount of yeast to be produced in a short time. What factors influence the growth of yeast? Does budding occur if the yeast is placed in salt solution instead of sugar solution? Do buds form if yeast is placed in vinegar? Beer? Baking soda solution? Alcohol? Apple juice?

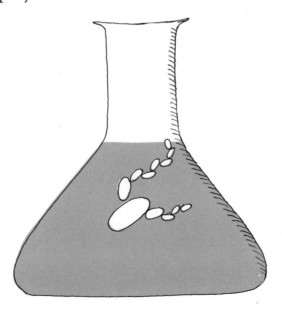

MILK

Bromcresol purple is an indicator which changes color when the acidity or alkalinity of a solution changes. What is observed if vinegar is added to a solution of bromcresol purple? If sodium bicarbonate is added? What happens to the color of bromcresol purple when it is added to milk and then allowed to stand at room temperature for several days?

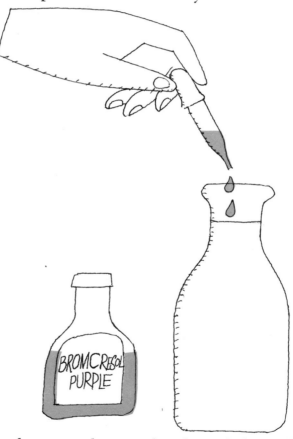

Does the same change take place if the milk with bromcresol purple is kept refrigerated?

More can be learned about what happens to the milk by observing the effects of various chemicals on milk. Compare the results obtained by warming a mixture of milk and rennet powder, an enzyme, with those obtained by warming just milk. What is seen if bromcresol purple is added to each of these?

What changes are seen if vinegar is added to a mixture of milk and bromcresol purple? Does adding baking soda instead of vinegar have the same effect?

DECOMPOSITION

What happens to a dead insect, a leaf, wool, cotton, rubber, plastic and nylon when they are pressed into the surface of rich garden soil and allowed to remain there for several weeks?

What happens if beach sand or construction sand is used instead of garden soil?

What effect does covering the pots with transparent plastic have?

Imagine that nothing in the world ever rotted or was decomposed. Would that be good or bad? It might be good because wooden fence posts would never have to be replaced, there would be no need for food preservatives, and there would be no putrid odor from garbage dumps. But if decomposition did not take place, that odorless garbage dump might be five miles high, lakes would be full of dead plants and animals, and a safari across the African veldt would have to thread its way through the intact carcasses of millions of dead elephants.

What causes decomposition? What happens to a dead insect, a leaf and pieces of wool, cotton, rubber, plastic and nylon that are placed in rich garden soil that has first been baked in an oven for several hours?

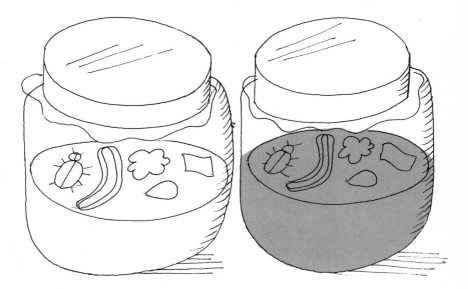

What occurs if the objects are placed on baked soil that has been moistened with boiled water?

ROTTEN EGGS

Is there a characteristic odor produced by the action of bacteria on eggs?

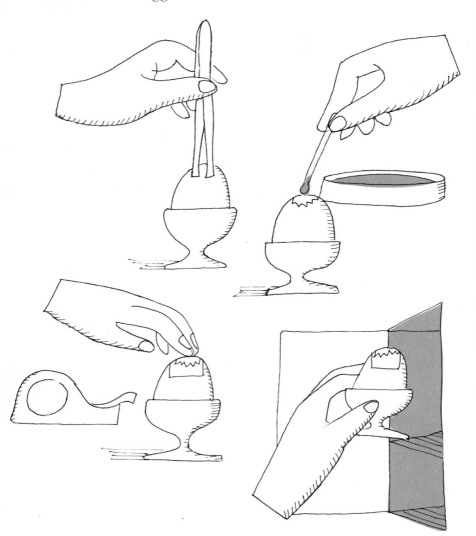

Can the same odor be detected if meat, milk, apple juice, mashed potatoes or other foods are inoculated with bacteria?

How long must the food be incubated before an odor is noticeable?

What substance is present in eggs but not in other foods that may be responsible for the unique odor produced? To answer this question, a chemist would perform a number of tests. One such test can be done in a simplified form by inserting a solid silver dime into each of the foods. What color changes can be observed on the dime if this is done? Do those foods that produce the color change also produce the unique odor? What would a chemist do with this kind of information? He might look for a known substance that produces the same effects.

What happens to a dime that is placed in a solution of sulfur and water?

THE GROWTH CURVE

How rapidly does the population of yeast cells in a medium increase? This question can be answered by adding equal amounts of yeast to tubes of medium at hourly intervals. Does the medium have to be sterilized? Apple juice can be used as the medium. Is it helpful to keep one tube uninoculated? What differences can be observed in all the tubes 24 hours after the first one has been inoculated? Does holding the tubes in front of newsprint aid in determining what has occurred?

Can a number be given to express how much growth has occurred? The numbered series of colors in the illustration may be helpful in measuring what has occurred. What type of line results when the "color values" are charted against time?

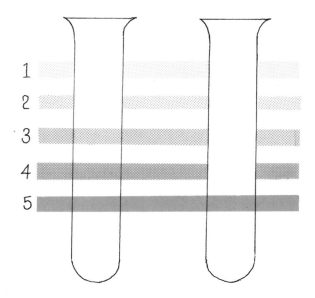

Can the line that represents growth be used to find out when the population stops increasing?

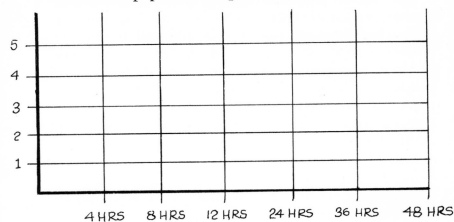

Is it possible that the population of yeast cells in a culture can continue to increase indefinitely? For example, under optimum growth conditions, yeast cells may divide every thirty minutes. At this rate, starting with one yeast cell, we would have after

½ hour—2 yeast cells
1 hour—4 yeast cells
2 hours—16 yeast cells

The formula that expresses this relationship is $N = 2^n$, where N equals the number of yeast cells and n equals the number of divisions. For instance, in two hours, four divisions would have occurred. Substituting in the formula, we get

$$N = 2^4 = 2 \times 2 \times 2 \times 2 = 16$$

What would be the population after eight hours? After one day? One week? Why isn't the earth covered with yeast cells?

VITAMINS

Do microbes need vitamins? If so, how much do they need? Is it possible for microbes to have "too much of a good thing"? What growth rate occurs if bacteria are cultured in pure water to which dextrose has been added? What effect on growth is seen if vitamins are added to the dextrose solution? Does varying the concentration of vitamins affect growth? A vitamin solution can be made by grinding a multiple vitamin tablet in a little water.

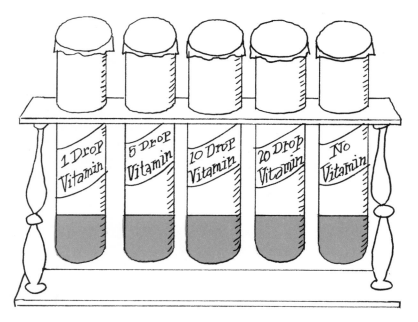

Should the solution be capped and sterilized before the bacteria are added? A very small amount of bacteria from a colony in "Soil—Home for Millions" can be used in this study.

What is the relationship between the amount of dextrose and the amount of bacterial growth? Between the amount of vitamins and bacterial growth?

TUBE	AMOUNT DEXTROSE	AMOUNT VITAMIN SOLUTION	AMOUNT WATER	AMOUNT GROWTH
1	0 drops	0 drops	2 tblsp	?
2	5 drops	0 drops	2 tblsp	?
3	10 drops	0 drops	2 tblsp	?
4	20 drops	0 drops	2 tblsp	?
5	0 drops	2 drops	2 tblsp	?
6	0 drops	5 drops	2 tblsp	?
7	0 drops	20 drops	2 tblsp	?
8	10 drops	2 drops	2 tblsp	?
9	10 drops	5 drops	2 tblsp	?
10	10 drops	20 drops	2 tblsp	?

Are line values useful in determining the amount of bacterial growth? Can a graph based on this information be used in finding out how much vitamin material there is in an unknown mixture?

SOURCES OF MATERIALS

Your kitchen and medicine cabinet
Sugar and spice and other things nice, such as:

Aluminum foil
Baking soda
Beef bouillon cubes
Detergent, powder or liquid
Eggs
Fungicide (powder for treating athlete's foot)
Gelatin powder
Iodine solution
Molasses
Mouthwash (any brand)
Paraffin
Rubbing alcohol
Starch
Table salt
Tomato juice
Vinegar
Vitamins, drops or pills
Yeast pellets
Yogurt

Laboratory supply company (*Items marked with asterisk may sometimes be found in hobby shops)

Agar
Bromcresol purple
*Calcium hydroxide (for making limewater)
*Corks to fit test tubes
*Crystal violet powder
*Glass slides, 1" x 3"

*Litmus paper, blue
*Litmus paper, red
*Methylene blue powder
Petri plates, 100 mm
Phenol (also called carbolic acid) CAUTION!
Phenol is harmful to the skin. Read and follow
directions on the bottle carefully.
*Sulfur powder
*Test tubes, pyrex, 16 x 150 mm

Aquarium supply or pet supply store

Elodea, a water plant.

Reference book

Needham & Needham, A *Guide to the Study of
Freshwater Biology.* San Francisco, Holden-Day,
1962.

GLOSSARY

AGAR   Agar is a carbohydrate obtained from certain seaweeds. It is used to solidify, or gel, growth media.

ANAEROBE   An organism that is able to live and grow in the absence of oxygen is called an anaerobe.

ANTIBIOTIC   Any substance produced by microbes that inhibits the growth of other microbes is called an antibiotic.

BUDDING   Budding is a special form of fission in which a new cell is formed from an existing cell. The new cell is smaller than the parent cell and remains attached for some time.

CULTURE   A group of organisms grown in a single container is called a culture. The word culture can also be used to describe the procedures used to grow microbes.

ENZYME   Enzymes are specialized proteins, produced by an organism, that control the rates of chemical reactions.

FISSION   Fission is a process by which cells reproduce. It involves the division of a cell to form two new cells.

FUNGICIDE   A fungicide is a substance that kills fungi.

GERMICIDE Any chemical that kills "germs" is called a germicide. If the "germs" being killed happen to be bacteria, the chemical is called a *bactericide*.

INCUBATE The process of keeping microbes in a favorable environment so that growth will occur is called incubation.

INDICATOR A substance which changes color when conditions of a reaction change is called an indicator.

INHIBITION The prevention of growth by chemical or physical means is called inhibition.

INOCULATE The process of introducing microbes into a growth medium is called inoculation.

MEDIUM The mixture of substances in which microbes grow is called the medium. This mixture contains food and other essential materials.

MICROBE Any organism that is too small to be seen by the unaided eye is called a microbe. Included in this group are bacteria, viruses, protozoa, algae and some fungi.

MICROORGANISM *See* microbes.

OPTIMUM TEMPERATURE The temperature at which a microbe grows most readily is called the optimum temperature. This temperature varies with the species.

PASTEURIZATION   The process of treating milk and other liquids in order to reduce the number of live bacteria present is called pasteurization.

pH   A symbol used by scientists to report the degree of acidity or alkalinity of a solution. A solution that is neither acidic nor alkaline is called neutral, and its pH is 7. If a solution is acidic, its pH is less than 7—if it is basic, its pH is greater than 7.

PURE CULTURE   A pure culture is one that contains only a single species of microbe.

RADIANT ENERGY   Any energy that comes from a radiating source is called radiant energy. Some examples of radiating sources are the sun, electric light bulbs and electric heating elements. Examples of radiant energy include visible light, ultraviolet, X rays, radio waves and infrared light.

SMEAR   A thin film of microbes spread over a microscope slide is called a smear.

STERILIZATION   Any process that is used to remove or destroy microbes is called sterilization. Methods of sterilization include heating, chemical treatment and filtering.

SUSPENSION   A suspension is a mixture of microbes in a liquid. Suspensions may be made in water, growth medium or any other liquid. In suspensions, particles do not dissolve, but are suspended, and eventually they settle to the bottom.

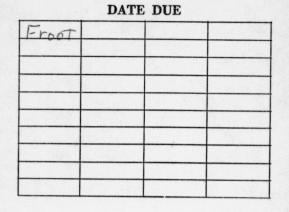